Love Don't Come Easy

The Modern Struggle

Fattima Mahdi

About The Author

Fattima is a 25-year-old writer, lyricist and professional roller-skater. With a BSc in Psychology, she has also spent a lot of her time mentoring young adults in London, Malta, Panama and South Africa.

As an advocate of self-development, Fattima works alongside Truth Theory, an online magazine that has over 1.5 million followers. She has also featured on VICELAND's docu-series *Jungletown* and has performed at the Barbican art gallery in Eddie Peake's live installation, *The Forever Loop.*

Music: www.soundcloud.com/msfatz
Blog: www.thoughtsfromthebalcony.wordpress.com

Acknowledgements

I wish to acknowledge Dami Afolabi for his creative efforts. Without him, this book would not have been possible. I also wish to thank Kamran Assadi for his inspired editorial guidance and my partner Kwame Johnson-Goffe for his continued support.

Contents

"You've got him deep into your soul,

Always free and never sold,

But that new puss, it soon becomes old,

And that new story soon becomes told,

'Cos love don't,

No love don't come easy"

Fattima Mahdi

1. Introduction

We are the generation raised on Google, YouTube and Facebook. We spend the majority of our time scrolling through newsfeeds, uploading pictures on Instagram and creating stories on Snapchat. Social media is an integral part of our lives and as a result, it also plays an important role in our relationships. Before we enter into a relationship, we first need to be attracted to the person. What makes somebody attractive to you? What sparks a connection? There is so much pressure to envision whom we want to be with and the attributes we want them to have. We are constantly being asked what our type is and quite frankly we do not always know the answer. Once we start dating, how do we interact with the person we are interested in? How can traditionalist views in relation to rules and regulations affect a new romantic relationship? For example, is the 90-day rule really effective in keeping that guy or girl you like interested?

It is clear that we have become more and more concerned with how we are perceived online. How have apps like Instagram changed our perceptions of self-worth? What impact does this have on our self-esteem and how can this subconsciously inhibit our ability to grow and sustain romantic connections? Relationships have changed. Traditional values that were once attributed to marriage are no longer seen in the same light. Many of my friends have seen their parents get divorced and this has deterred them from getting married and making similar mistakes. Some of my friends are wholly career-orientated and see marriage and children as something they will eventually make time for, one day. The days of falling in love at 17, getting married at 21 and spending the rest of your life with the woman or man of your dreams, have long since passed. We have socially evolved. Given the prevalence of technology and common social media platforms, this comes as no surprise. For one, the ways in which we approach someone we find attractive tends to involve a scroll and a swipe on apps such as Tinder and Plenty of Fish. This has also given rise to the hook-up culture. With so many online dating sites, it is easier than ever to fulfill those burning desires – even if it is just for one night. The Mistress now operates under a new name – the Side Chick, and the many definitions of cheating have grown even longer still. For example, some of us categorically class *Likes* and *Comments* on certain Instagram or Facebook profiles as causes for concern.

In light of online interactions, our perceptions of what it means to be in love are also changing. We have extended our definitions of love to accommodate the new ways we can display it. For example, an *In a Relationship* status on Facebook is a new way some of us validate the true meaning of love. Not changing your *Single* status on Facebook but claiming that you love someone can raise a few eyebrows. Similarly, not displaying affection online, by means of taking and uploading Selfies with your partner, can mean that you do not feel the way you say you do. If you did, you would let your friends and followers see it too.

Having an online and offline persona creates pressure to conflate the two. It is clear that a new language of love has been formulated. For my generation, this is certainly a conversation worth having.

2. What's Your Flavour?

What's your type? Everyone appears to have one. So what's yours? Is a type even important? Surely, there are a ton of people we omit based on a checklist construed by some sort of external ideal of what our 'type' should be. Do these confined rules deter us from meeting someone who could be our better half and, instead, draw us closer to someone who may in fact be terribly bad for us? This is an important question because it will determine some, if not all, of our relationships.

We are all attracted to certain personality traits and as a result, we are attracted to people who possess them. We can be drawn to people who have a sense of adventure, people who play hard to get, as well as people who are open-minded and funny. We constantly read other people's behaviour, perceive their actions and formulate expectations. Some men have a natural appeal and will have no issues getting women; other men are repelled at all costs.

It is important to note, that what we look for in a relationship may also be heavily influenced by what we see online. First impressions are everything. To-day, those impressions are made based on our social media activity. We can screen our potential partners online and if we don't like what we see, they may never be shortlisted for the first date. Even if we initially meet someone offline, we can still go home and check out their online persona, to get a feel for who they 'really' are. For us women, maybe we don't want him to have too many female followers as this implies he is a bit of a ladies man. For men, the women they are sizing up may seem more appealing if they have a lot of male attention on Instagram. This means that our online personas can hold significant weight, often influencing whether or not we choose to move forward with the relationship.

What Do Women Want?

A question that has been on many men's lips for years is – what do women want? Let's be honest ladies, we can be confusing beings, and we don't always know what we want until it's right in front of us. For example, I was once good friends with a guy, who at face value, I didn't think I was attracted to. However, as time went on, I got to know him better and he began to appeal to me in more ways than one. From confident, intellectual, to sensitive and romantic, it appears that there are some clear common male typologies that women gravitate towards.

- **Mr. Confident, not Cocky**

He is assertive, secure in himself and knows what he wants, as a result, he has clear career goals that he plans on making a reality.

- **Mr. Intellectual**

He loves to engage in conversations that exceed the norm. He can spend hours debating with his woman about various worldly issues. I believe that an intellectual connection plays a significant role in the longevity of a relationship, as being able to stay interested above and beyond the physical level is more likely to keep you invested.

- **Mr. Romantic**

He is the epitome of romance and often opens doors for his woman and brings her flowers. He wants to show his her that he cares, which is why he puts effort into ensuring that she is treated like a queen.

- **Mr. Nice Guy**

This man is affectionate and sensitive to his partner's feelings. He asks her out on various dates and always pays, even when she demands to split the bill. Most men assume that women do not want a nice guy. However, many women have experienced bad relationships, so, the nice guy normally wins in the end.

What (Some) Women End Up With

So now you have a shortlist of what women want, however, these are not always the types of men that women end up in a relationship with. There seems to be some discrepancies between a woman's ideal partner and a woman's actual partner. It is easy to get caught up in the idea of love, especially when it feels like we have been searching for the one we want forever. Sometimes, we get desperate and settle for the one that will do.

- **Mr. Flosser**

This guy always looks sharp. His dress sense is better than hers (at least that is what he thinks). He drives a nice car, takes her out to nice restaurants, pays for everything and keeps her pampered. But, money is his solution to every problem, so he uses his wealth to win arguments and to claim her as his property.

- **Mr. Tooth Ache**

This fine chiseled man is under no illusion - he knows he's 'all that'. How? Because everyone tells him so! All the ladies flirt with him, saying how sweet he is and he effortlessly flirts back. They'll giggle; they'll even hug him when he is with his girlfriend. But, he only has eyes for her... or so he says. Let's face it ladies, we all want to be with someone that others find attractive, but he knows that other women want him, so he may not want to commit to a long-term relationship.

• Mr. Golden Tongue

Mr. Golden Tongue is my personal favourite. He can talk himself out of every situation. If there were an award for being the smoothest talker, Mr. G.T. would win it. Women hang on his every word because he is so good at feeding them those sweet nothings. Our friends do it too. They talk about leaving that job they can't stand or that guy they have had enough of. However, years have passed, and yes, they are still in that same role, moaning about that same job and cursing out that same guy they were meant to leave. Ladies, Mr. G.T. can talk all he wants, however, what is he doing to show you that he loves you? Actions always have, and always will speak louder than words. Remember that.

• Mr. Prize Possession

Sometimes a woman can end up with a trophy boyfriend, you know, someone she can show off to her friends. He isn't really relationship material, but she will play along for now, just to see what the high life with him is like.

What Men Do Not Want

- **Miss Jealous**

This woman is always on edge. She has been cheated on in the past and as a result, any man she meets will have to pay for the sins of his predecessor. She questions if he is being faithful at all times and keeps tabs on him as a means of dealing with her insecurities. A lot of my male friends have suffered at the hands of jealous women. One friend in particular was constantly being accused of infidelity. He pleaded his innocence on many occasions and tried his best to reassure her. Sadly, the lack of trust did not simmer and he had no choice but to end the relationship altogether.

- **Miss Fixer**

Miss Fixer thinks that it is her God-given right to 'fix' her man. She is quick to point out his flaws and is determined to mold him in a way that suits her needs - starting with his music, his dress sense and then his career choices. The list is endless! She says that it is *"for his own good"* and that she *"only wants the best for him"*, which probably has elements of truth in it. However, if her man was to try and change her in this way – she will scream at the top of her lungs about having independence and being accepted for who she is.

Let's Be Real

As our life experiences begin to shape us, our 'type' is likely to change over time. Whom we want now may not be whom we want in the future. For example, perhaps you are at a stage in your life where you only have time for something short term, and would prefer a Mr. or Mrs. Right Now. Somebody you can chill with, without the expectation of it progressing into a serious relationship. Or, maybe you've been there, done that, and now you're determined to find 'the one'. As a result, you often dismiss those who fail to measure up to your high standard, adamant that a better version of them will come along.

Ladies, if you are waiting for your Mr. Right, aka Mr. Doctor - who is between the ages of 22-25 years old, is 6ft 2inches in height, has a honey-nut complexion and earns more than £40,000 a year - you really are limiting your options. You do not have to lessen your standards, just be a bit more open to the choices available. Even if you do come across Mr. Honey Nut Doctor, who is to say that he is looking in your direction? Perhaps, he is looking for a 5ft 8inch model with a 22-inch waist and unfortunately, you do not fit the bill.

3. There Are No Rules!

When it comes to dating, some of us like to enforce all sorts of rules, regulations and self-made legislations that must be adhered to, never to be deviated from for any reason whatsoever. Do not pay for your half of the bill (even though you ate half of the food), do not call them for three days and certainly do not sleep with them for 90 days. These are ridiculous outdated rules, which create the ideology that if all couples use generalised behaviour 'X', then it will lead to outcome 'Y' and their relationship will be successful. It is never that simple.

Half!

Women have fought long and hard, and are still fighting, to be seen as equals in society. However, when it comes to paying for the first date, a lot of women think men should be courteous and foot the bill. Once upon a time, men were clear breadwinners and women were merely housewives. Today, women are far more independent and career-orientated and can certainly afford to chip in. So, what's the hold up? For some women, whether or not the date went well is dependent on whether or not their date paid for the bill. The prospect of a second date is hanging in the balance. Yes, the actual balance, printed right at the bottom of the receipt. He could have wooed her, struck up a good conversation but if he didn't offer to pay, she will instantly be turned off.

Dating apps have changed the game and we are now going on dates by the dozen. Unfortunately, this means that men are expected to pay for a lot more first dates than they used to. This is a shame because I feel that the quality of the date is dependent on the conversation, not the financial dynamic. I have been on dates and paid half or offered to pay and the man has insisted on paying. Of course, it's a nice gesture, a bit of traditional charm, but it's not a requirement. It doesn't form my opinion of them, because it's the 21st century and I am trying to move away from patriarchal values.

The Call Game

"When should I call?" In my opinion, women are far more analytical and calculated than men when it comes to this trivial dilemma. Am I missing something? Is there a formula that has been designed specifically for deciding on when or when not to call someone you have just started dating? Let's see, if I

multiply the first date by three days, minus the text he sent me yesterday, that equals call him. Really? So much time and energy is spent calculating when to call because we do not want to come across as desperate. There is no script - you are not actors or actresses and this is not a feature film. Ladies, if he is on your mind one day and you want to call him, then why hold back for fear of appearing too forward? Just pick up the phone.

In the event that the newly formed relationship does not work out as planned, 'playing it cool' is often a defense mechanism that some of us use to ensure that our feelings are protected. For example, I have friends who make up excuses as to why they cannot spend time with someone they're seeing, when all they want to do is just that. They will decline invitations to go out and sit at home watching brain-cell-killing Friday night TV because they don't want their love interest to think that they are always available.

Challenging the 90-Day Rule

I have nothing against American comedian, actor, author and radio personality, Steve Harvey. However, after watching his movie *Think Like a Man (2012)*, I found myself questioning his dating and relationship advice. If you have seen the film, then you will know that it encourages women to adopt a male approach - hence the title - when trying to hold down a long-term relationship. There are a number of strategic games that the women are encouraged to play and there is also an exhaustive list of rules that they are told to enforce. One of these is the 90-Day Rule. Though Steve did not coin this rule, it is through his film that it came to resonate with me. According to Steve, I am under strict instruction to make my man wait 90 days before allowing him to 'get the cookie'. Why would waiting 90 days express anything other than the fact that you are counting down the days to when you can be intimate with your partner? Who even decided that 90 days was the sufficient amount of time needed? There are 7,776,000 seconds in 90 days, what makes this amount of time so special?

In my opinion, the 90-Day Rule is flawed because it determines the pace and the progression of your relationship. In the event that you are not ready to have sex on the 90th day, are you still obligated to give it up, as this was the initial agreement? The answer should of course be no. However, I know women who have succumbed to the act solely because they felt that they had made the man "*wait long enough*". Some even said, "*he could have tried to get in my panties but he didn't*". In this instance, the 90-Day Rule makes sex a commodity, nothing more than a transaction for behaving as expected. Sex - in my eyes - is an expression of love and devotion, not a reward for good behavior. Rather than trying to make it to the 90th day, you should enjoy each other's company and be sexually intimate when you both know the time is right.

The 90-Day Rule is also seen as a good way of teasing apart the 'keepers' from the 'leavers'. However, it is important to note that it does not necessarily categorise good and bad guys. There will be some men who jump ship after hearing the duration they have to wait. However, others could easily adopt a 'challenge accepted' kind of attitude - in which they wait it out, complete the mission and get the 'prize' at the end of it. To put it bluntly, if he so wishes, a man can decide that he only intends on having sex, wait 90 days, do the deed and still leave. How do I know this? A friend of mine used the 90-Day Rule and that is exactly what happened to her. As soon as she had sex with him, he broke off all forms of contact. You see, the 90-Day Rule only promotes game play from the start and two can play that game!

For some of you reading this, the 90-Day Rule is probably going to be a good way of abstaining from sex. However, whether or not the rule is effective in cultivating stable long-term relationships is still debatable. I will never use a stringent rule to dictate my sex life because sex is not meant to be a calculated event, planned on a timeline. It is supposed to be spontaneous, meaningful and intuitive. Sorry Steve, but I will not be 'thinking like a man'. Instead, I will be thinking like a woman and trusting my instincts, not rules.

4. Self-Esteem

Self-esteem is a critical component needed for a healthy and loving relationship. When we feel secure in ourselves, we can be open, vulnerable and love unconditionally. However, being over-critical in our self-analysis can have a negative effect on the romantic relationships we form.

People with low self-esteem might avoid intimacy, refusing to connect on a deeper level, for fear of being hurt. On the other hand, they might entertain destructive relationships that lack satisfaction. Due to the fact that they doubt their ability to make good decisions, they might also let their partner make the decisions on their behalf. Or worse still, they act as a magnet, attracted to people who treat them the way that they feel about themselves. Some people with low self-esteem are also good at sabotaging perfectly healthy relationships. For example, their partner may treat them with respect. However, they choose to focus all of their energy on the negatives. *"Why would they want to be with me. Are they cheating? They must be cheating. There is no way this relationship is working out. It just can't be. Something must be going on!".* Perhaps, a previous relationship ended badly and that left them feeling unwanted and insignificant. As a result, they are unable to fully trust their partner and need constant reassurance. Furthermore, some people with low self-esteem will latch onto anyone who appears to like them. Even if it means entering into a relationship with someone who is insensitive, disrespectful or abusive. Does this sound like you? If so, I'm here to tell you that you don't need to be in a relationship to be seen as valuable. If you decide to be with someone solely for a self-esteem boost, you are likely to attract partners who will exploit you. They will be able to get away with things that should be addressed head on because you'll downplay or shrug off their actions. If you do not respect yourself, then how can you be seen as an equal in a relationship? You should never go above and beyond for someone who would rarely, if ever, do the same for you.

I Cannot Compete

If you don't quite feel secure in your relationship, ensuring that your partner remains focused on you can be an anxious exercise. They are constantly being exposed to beautiful men and women. On the street, in their workplace and, more importantly, on their smartphone. With the ever-growing use of social media, trying to keep your partner's eyes on you and off of apps like Instagram and Snapchat can be extremely difficult. The potential number of people vying for their attention behind the screen could be infinite. Your partner could be interacting with said girls or guys online - lusting over their Instagram-filtered Selfies and provocative poses. These emerging online ideals are causing many of us to view ourselves in a different light. We now question whether or not we are good enough for our significant other. Why? Because we know that we can't compete with "SweetCandyThighs" or "JuliusEightPack" who have over 10,000 Instagram followers and effortlessly rack up thousands of *Likes* per post. There is now a threat to the relationship with every scroll and swipe and we have little to no control over it. In a desperate attempt to see what our partner is getting up to online, some of us have gone as far as creating pseudo-profiles to spy on our partner's followers. Don't worry, I will touch on this later.

Being Confident

Be confident enough to be yourself. If you want a committed relationship, say so. Do not settle for a fling. Being too eager to please at your own expense, will not be worth it in the long run. Being confident means that you do not have to second-guess yourself or change your values to suit his or her needs. Being confident means you do not let the relationship progress too far without addressing any major concerns that you have. It also means that you do not hesitate to talk to your significant other about something that is bothering you. Being confident means that you focus less on other people's relationships and you concentrate on your own. Being confident means you can be you and being you is important.

It's All About You

Sometimes, the hardest person to love is yourself. We see people around us who reflect our ideal self, then wonder why we don't have the job we want or why we can't attract the guy or girl we like so much. It's frustrating and can leave us feeling depressed and alone. You should constantly strive to be a better version of yourself. Find ways to achieve your dreams; don't just be upset because other people are doing something you wish you had the courage to do. It doesn't matter how many times we fail, it only matters if we stop trying. The road to success is never easy but it starts with loving yourself, your flaws and everything else in between. You are not perfect and you never will be. But if you just take the time to work on yourself, to grow, to thrive, to succeed, you will realise that you can achieve more than you ever thought was possible.

5. Relationship Dilemmas

Do you have a friend who has let you know, in one way or another, that their intentions are not platonic? Are you currently seeing someone and wondering why they won't commit? Do you want your partner to stop being so controlling? Are you in a long distance relationship, and now you're not quite sure if you can actually go the distance? Relationships are tricky. They are often confusing, complicated and can lead to a whirlwind of emotions. There are many common relationship dilemmas that can arise, so, whether you are single and still looking, or in fact taken, it is important that you are prepared to handle them. Otherwise, you may find yourself struggling to deal with a sticky situation.

Just A Friend?

Is it possible to preserve the harmony in your relationship whilst maintaining a friendship with someone of the opposite sex? Well, if this is a friend whom you have known since nursery, your partner will just have to get over it. However, if this is a friend whom you have previously dated, your partner may not be comfortable with this arrangement. You cannot be angry with them for having a hard time accepting a friend of this nature. If you plan on keeping the peace, you will have to cut them out and fast. Furthermore, if this is a friend who is always messaging you and flirting with you any chance they get, then you need to stop and think about what is going on. If there are certain aspects of your friendship that you wouldn't feel comfortable disclosing with your partner then this is an issue. Remember, a friend who is interested in you may persist irrespective of the fact that you are in a relationship. If you continue to tolerate their behavior, rather than discourage it, then you could put your relationship in jeopardy.

Ladies, if you're feeling unsettled about the amount of female friends your man has, see how he interacts with them. He should want you to meet them. If he has no intention of you ever meeting his female friends, then elevate your right hand and wave that red flag. If his friendships are innocent, then there should be no problem. I wouldn't feel comfortable with my partner having so-called female friends I have never met. Uh uh, not me. It all comes down to trust. If he does not feel comfortable introducing me to them, then there will be an element of doubt in my mind about the nature of his friendships.

3 Ways To Friend Zone

Do you have a friend who makes subtle advances, hugs you for a fraction of a second too long and always laughs at your jokes, even when they are not funny? Having a friend like this can be difficult to deal with, especially when you're in a relationship. So how do you let them know that you're not interested without hurting their feelings? Here's how you can kindly open the door, nudge them inside, lock it and password protect it with the one-time only friend zone code.

- **Tell Them They Are A Good Friend**

Ignore the blatant comments they make about you being in a romantic relationship together and reiterate how much of a good friend they are. Make sure they know the value of your friendship - this may make them second-guess their attempts at winning your heart.

- **Avoid Physical Contact**

Don't kiss their cheek, hug them or hold hands. Nada! It might seem harsh but if they have feelings for you, this will only give them ammunition to pursue you further. Decline offers to go to the cinema, out for dinner or anything else that has a slight romantic undertone.

- **Talk About Other Love Interests**

In order to maintain a good friendly relationship tell them about your life dramas and talk about your boyfriend, girlfriend or someone you're interested in as often as you can.

Wanting More

Just because a man and a woman are strictly friends, does not mean that they cannot progress to a romantic relationship. Some of us have probably found the man or woman of our dreams but they just happen to be our friend. Why is the friend zone so hard to emerge from? Why do we not want to date our friends? Sure, they know a hell of a lot about us; they have been around for some time and have witnessed our past relationships. Is that such a bad thing? Sometimes, we remain friends because there is a restriction that permits us from being more than that. Such as, he previously dated one of our friends, or perhaps she is currently in a relationship. If these restrictions were not in place, then the chances are that we would have pursued something more than just a friendship. Fellas - if you like her, just tell her. I cannot say she will feel the same way, but at least you would have got it off your chest. The same goes for you ladies - you can be friendzoned too! Life is too short to have *what-ifs*, be free from regret and just be honest with your feelings.

My Brother and Male Friends

My brother has no trouble wooing the ladies, however, he often feels trapped when they start to express too much interest in him. He once described a time when a woman he 'hung out' with started texting him constantly, asking him what he was up to and making advanced plans. He told me that she was acting as if they were already in a relationship and this made him feel claustrophobic. As a result, he felt that he had no choice but to break off all forms of communication with her. I think there are quite a few men who have this problem, they like the idea of having a relationship but not the effort and exclusivity that goes with it. My male friends tell me all the time that they are 'hanging out' with a woman, not dating her. I happen to think these terms mean the same thing, but men can be very good at choosing words that exonerate them from commitment. He may have taken her out for a meal and a long walk in the park, but in his eyes, this is not a date. What he fails to do is relay this information to her, causing confusion between them.

A lot of women see intimacy as signs of a blossoming relationship. However, a lot of men want intimacy without having to take on the responsibility of a committed relationship. Men, please let your thoughts mirror your actions and stop having sex with women you don't like. Ladies, if you are looking for commitment and he is not showing signs of wanting a relationship, why is your bra, let alone your panties, dropping to the floor for him? It is important that you are both on the same page and want the same things. There needs to be a consensus in order to minimise the chances of heartache later on down the line. When we fail to communicate, we end up with a large grey area where we try to infer what the other is thinking. This is hard work and not conducive to a good working relationship. This should go without saying but it is astonishing how few people effectively communicate their needs.

He's Not Ready

Ladies, if you have been 'seeing' a guy for quite some time and still have not received that important promotion to full-time girlfriend, then chances are you never will. When faced with the classic *"so where is this going?"* talk, some men know how to squirm their way out of making an outright commitment. The words *"I'm happy with the way things are"* is a common response from those that do not want to proceed to the next level of their relationship. He keeps stringing you along, telling you that he just needs more time, but all the while, he is enjoying the perks of having you as a girlfriend without actually being your boyfriend. Sound familiar? We sometimes think that guys are just being macho about their feelings. I guess those are the lies we tell ourselves to reassure us that he feels the way we do. When a man says he is not having sex with anyone else apart from you, he means he is not having sex with anyone else apart from you. Some women will translate this to *"you are my girlfriend"*, but that is not what he said. If he wanted you to be his girlfriend - he would have said those exact words. Full stop! The fact of the matter is that we like to give men the benefit of the doubt. There is a common misconception that he will take the plunge and assert his position as the man in our life if we 'give him time.' If you are ready for something serious and he isn't, then as much as this may hurt, he is not the one for you. Though he possesses some exceptional qualities, there is a major detail that cannot be overlooked here. He is just not ready for a committed relationship. It's easy to get caught up trying to please him, in the hopes that he will change his mind, however, investing in this fantasy means that you are short-changing yourself. The issue is that you never know if he will ever commit. You could wait nine years and still not get what you want. He has openly stated that he isn't ready and the chances of that changing are unlikely, especially if you are already having casual sex. Think about it. Would you offer to pay rent on a house you have been given the option of living in for free? It is very easy to get caught up and lose sight of the bigger picture. I cannot even begin to count the amount of times my friends have been hurt in the past because they misinterpreted the terms and conditions of their relationship, or lack thereof.

What's the Hold Up?

You spend a lot of time together and constantly interact on WhatsApp, Instagram and Snapchat. You do not have an anniversary date, so technically it is not official - but as far as you're concerned, everything else is akin to a committed and loving relationship. Are you not in some ways together even though this has not been discussed? Isn't it funny that if we do not identify what we are with someone, then somehow it appears less real and illegitimate? There are a number of reasons why both men and women shy away from labeling their relationships. If you are currently stuck in limbo, wondering why your relationship status remains unclear, then there could be deeper issues at play.

- **Their Ex Is In The Picture**

Are there a lot of pictures of their ex on Facebook? Did you meet soon after their break up? They might be keeping you at arms length because they still have feelings for their ex. You may think they are the one for you but do not overlook these details. It is better to get to the bottom of it sooner rather than later.

- **Can't Commit. Won't Commit**

As I previously mentioned, there are some people who do not want a serious relationship. Perhaps, other priorities are more prevalent in their life and they have no interest in making you a central component just yet. It does not matter how much you try and get them to commit, they are just not ready yet. Being in an official relationship means that they have to live up to it and the reality of that can be too much to bear.

• They Are Keeping Their Options Open

They may be trying to keep their options open and so they do not want to warrant you with exclusive access just yet. If things look like they are getting too serious, they may start spending less time alone with you and, instead, opt for group dates where you can enjoy activities together in a less date-like setting.

• Are You Being Too Forceful?

Are you trying to force the commitment too much? The very act of pressurising them to be with you can lead to resistance. Even if they are ready to commit to you, they may be thinking twice about it now. If you are already trying to control the situation, perhaps you will be even more controlling when in a fully committed relationship.

No Strings!

As I previously mentioned, some people are very career-orientated and simply don't have the time to meet the demands of a relationship. A No Strings

Attached (NSA) arrangement affords them the luxury of sexual intimacy at their convenience. They do not have to worry about arguments, emotions and the like... or do they? NSA arrangements have worked perfectly for some people and have gone disastrously wrong for others, so if you are considering a relationship of this nature, it is important that you know what you are getting yourself into.

Most people who engage in a NSA arrangement tend to do so with a friend, but before you go ahead and do this, you should be weary of how sex may change the dynamic of your friendship. Brace yourself, because once you do the deed, things can quickly become awkward. You might feel paranoid about appearing clingy and so you hang out with your friend less often. Or, you might be worried about how your friend will take the news that you want to end the agreement and date someone else. For example, a male friend of mine agreed to have a mutually exclusive NSA arrangement with a friend he had known for over 10 years, but then he started dating someone else who he really liked. This caused a lot of problems for his newly forming relationship and it also cost him his friendship.

Sex can lead to unexpected feelings. You might think that you have your emotions under control but once you are intimate, you're feelings towards them might get a little more complicated and this could put a serious strain on your friendship. For example, what do you do if you discover that you like your friend more than you thought you did and wish to pursue a romantic relationship that is not solely based on sex? How do you transition from one status to another? What if the other party does not wish to change the arrangement? There are so many complex questions and situations that a NSA agreement can bring. It hurts my head just thinking about it. This should go without saying, but some people forget that a NSA arrangement will end at some point. If this were not the case, then it would be a relationship. Therefore, if you are currently in, or seeking a NSA arrangement - you should know that your time has already been capped.

Deal Breakers

Have you ever really liked someone, only to find out that his ex is his best friend or that she has had too many male partners? Everyone has their own standards. No matter how much you like the person; there is that one thing that you know will never get easier with time. For some people - it could be their height; it may be their political views or their incessant bad breath. Encountering a deal breaker is like finding a cockroach in your food; it sends everyone running in the opposite direction.

- **The Serial Flirter**

They take being 'friendly' to a whole new level, over-complimenting your friends on their physique, starting conversations with strangers and copping a feel whenever they get a chance.

• Under Your Skin

They constantly criticise you and take every chance they get to belittle you and make hurtful comments about your aesthetics, character and personality.

• Public Humiliation

They embarrass you in front of your friends, scrutinise your every move and pass judgement on every mistake you make. This is a deafening alarm that he or she does not see you as an equal. All matters should always be handled privately; public humiliation should never be something you have to put up with from your peers, let alone your significant other.

• Liar Liar

Have you caught your partner out in a lie? They may have told you that they were at home one morning, but then you later find out they had gone shopping. This is a problem. If they are willing to lie about the small things, they may try and pull the wool over your eyes about the bigger, more important things. In addition, if you find that you have to elicit information out of them, as they only tell you on a 'need to know basis' then this is definitely a major cause for concern.

Power Struggle

As much as I would like to tell you all that the forces in a relationship are always equal, they are not. For some of us, our relationship is a competition. This occurs when we see our partner as the opposition and make every attempt to claim silent victories, using an invisible point system. In this instance, being right all the time and winning can seem more important than being in love and building a strong unit with each other. I don't believe that relationships should be about being top of the leaderboard. Instead, it is about being a team, where both parties are happy and work together, not against each other. So, what happens when heads clash and you meet someone who is too much like you - too overpowering or confident, drawing attention away from you? If you are a couple who both feel that you need to lead, then I am afraid you are going to have to swallow some pride in order to reach a common ground. A relationship isn't about demanding your terms; it's about compromise. Having said that, there are instances in which we refuse to compromise. We want to have it our way and we will be the out-of-control toddler sprawled all over the shop floor, kicking and screaming, if it means that we can momentarily regain power in the relationship.

There is going to be a shift in power from time to time because both of you will want to feel like the superior one. For example, when on a date, the man might let the woman pick the restaurant. This will give the woman the perception that she has the power. He probably doesn't mind which place they are going to, but allowing her to choose, grants her superiority. Equally, a woman might allow her man to make a big decision on their behalf. This is a healthy power shift, a reciprocal act that allows both parties to lead. However, this does not mean that you should trade your power for their love and affection and nor should they you.

Not all power shifts are healthy. If you have to be in a full blown submissive state in order for your partner to love you, then you could be in trouble. For example, a friend of mine confessed that he used to have really long hair, which he cut off, simply because his girlfriend told him to. Although he was reluctant to shave it, he wan-ted her to be happy. You know the saying "happy wife, happy life". If only that were the case. She broke up with him a week later.

Going the Distance

Unless a firm foundation has been put in place, a long distance relationship will be very hard to maintain. This is not to say that it's impossible but the lack of face-to-face interaction will make it much harder to cultivate a strong connection. When you first start dating someone, you want to spend all of your time with them. If you happen to have met your significant other on a two-week holiday, then you might not be able to see them often. It can be frustrating, which, in turn can put a massive strain on the relationship. For example, at the early stages of your commitment, you might find it hard to trust your partner, after all, you don't know them that well and you don't get to see them often. If, after a few dates, you and your partner are many miles apart, you will probably drive yourself crazy. You'll be looking at all their social media updates, seeing all the fun they're having and wondering if they've ended up with someone else. They will do their best to reassure you, but it may not be enough.

Communication is integral to the longevity of any relationship, even more so when that relationship is long distance. Luckily, there are many ways you can talk to your significant other via WhatsApp, Facebook and the like. The list is endless. You're going to have to be inventive and pull out all the stops, making every effort to keep the conversation going. Use apps to play games, watch movies together and do anything else you can think of. If communicating becomes a chore and you find that you have a genuine lack of interest in the "*How's your week been?*" conversations, then it's likely your relationship will not last much longer. When infrequent interaction becomes the norm, it can result in diminished attraction towards your partner, which, in turn, increases the chances of you forming another relationship. If you're starting to have feelings for someone else, it's only a matter of time before looking leads to touching, spooning leads to forking and so on.

If you are in a long distance relationship then the future should be an important topic of discussion. You need to reach a unanimous decision on how you plan to proceed. Where is your relationship going? If you both plan on leading separate lives, in separate parts of the world, are you sure you'll be able to stay together forever? You may end up realising that you don't want to leave your home, they don't want to leave theirs and flights are really expensive.

To all the long distance couples reading this, it's not all doom and gloom, you can still make it against the odds. All you need is mutual trust, constant communication and the determination to stick together. In my opinion, some people use the distance as an excuse to 'call it quits' because it means less hassle. But if you really love someone you will find a way to be together, whether you are 5 or 50,000 miles apart.

6. Giving Your All

A healthy relationship is based on trust, honesty, respect, good communication and boundaries. Having the freedom to function as an individual, while in a relationship, will allow for personal growth. Can you survive without your partner? After all, they should be a significant addition to your life. Not your life. The desire to be loved is universal. Therefore, we all want someone to share our time with, whether it is a friend, family member or an intimate partner. However, if we are not careful, this natural tendency to love can lead to poor relationship choices.

In The Beginning

If you are in a relationship with someone who did not have any goals or aspirations before they met you, then they are unlikely to have them once they are with you. You can't really blame them for their lack of motivation and drive because you knew this from the beginning. For example, if they rely on handouts and favours from you, what chances are there that they will go on to fulfill a dream, any dream, especially now that they have you to help with their finances? You may think you are support- ing them, but watch out. They could be using you to build their own foundation or to simply go on living as they please. You may think that you are helping them to become a better person, but you are proba- bly just making them more dependable on you and less likely to excel. And besides, what are they doing for you? You are helping them with all these things and what are they doing to show you that they ap- preciate this? No. Sex does not count. Fine, he or she might be broke and you're okay with that - good for you. But what future ambitions are they actually working towards? Or, are they just sitting there tell- ing you about it, while eating at the fancy restaurant that you paid for yet again.

A Big Mistake

If you are in a dependent relationship and cannot function without your partner, this is neither healthy nor stable. Time apart is good. I know friends who will cancel plans they have made way in advance, so that they can spend time with their partner instead. Such dependency can also mean that you place the needs of your partner over your own. As a result, he or she is able to trample all over the boundaries that you set in the relationship, causing it to become toxic. Toxic relationships are bad. Really bad. They can leave one or both parties feeling physically and/or emotionally damaged. Another example of a toxic relationship, is one where there is a great deal of physical chemistry but you disagree on just about everything. You are morally and integrally different. When you fight, it gets ugly and can leave you both feeling exhausted. How-ever, you also have a deep physical attraction to your partner and cannot stay away. It is like taking an addictive drug and then dealing with the come down, day after day after day. Physically and mentally this relationship is the most draining.

Some of us just want to be loved. If we happen to meet someone who wants that too, we can fall into a trap. This can result in an exhausting relationship, where neither party really share any similar inter-ests, hobbies or passions but are determined to go the extra mile to make it work. This relationship looks great on the surface, but deep down there isn't really a connection. There is also a common miscon-ception that if we do what our partner wants, they will stay with us. This means changing how we so-cialise, how we dress and talk to suit our partner's needs. Remember my friend who cut off all of his hair? He allowed himself to lose all control in the re-lationship and instead just did everything his girl-friend told him. She eventually got bored of bossing him around and much like his hair, cut him off.

I Do Everything Around Here!

You make all the decisions. You cook, clean, plan all the dates and do just about everything else for them. Then, you get angry when they do not make an effort to reciprocate. Even though you have set the standard, you still want them to do more, without being asked to do so. It can be frustrating when you feel like you're giving your all, while they are just coasting through the relationship. This can create both a superiority and inferiority complex. On the one hand, you basically manage their life. On the other hand, you feel inferior because they do not pull their weight. You assume an executive position and they are merely your assistant... who doesn't really assist you. At first, doing so much seems natural. You are more than happy to cook for them and run their errands. However, once your relationship reaches a certain point, it dawns on you that your partner has not done much at all. As a result, you begin to feel more like their parent than their partner. You're breaking your back to make sure that they're happy and they're not even lifting a finger. And because you're investing every waking moment you have into the relationship, you have little time to reflect on yourself. But, what about you? What about what you want? You shouldn't have to wait on your partner hand and foot. A relationship is a partnership. If you are investing 90%, whereas, they are only investing 10%, then you need to redress the balance.

7. The Modern Struggle

We now seek more instant gratification than ever before. Everything can be upgraded. Perfectly good phones are discarded for a better model and TV is watched at our convenience, on anything but a TV! We want everything now. Right now. From my observations, I think this mentality has seeped into how we both perceive and subsequently interact in romantic relationships.

In this day and age, a relationship isn't something that is worked on. Divorce rates have sky rocketed in the past decade and this has changed our own perceptions of commitment. There is less pressure to maintain a stable relationship because it doesn't hold the same significance that it once did. Which, for me, is very disheartening. We have lost patience. Just like a phone has a use-by date, so do relationships. At the first sign of a fault, many of us just upgrade to a better model, someone who is not as much hassle. It seems easier to replace something, than take the time to repair it. With the modern world consumed by handheld devices, Tweets and

Facebook news feeds, it is also easier to find someone new. Apps like Tinder, Instagram and Snapchat give us the freedom to meet new people, within a few thumb taps. A simple swipe of the screen; a Follow or a Like and the broken relationships can be discarded, opposed to being nurtured and worked through – even through the bad times. All of this has given birth to the hook up culture. A culture in which two people who like each other enough, decide to have casual sex. They may even put a label on it because they want to keep enjoying the benefits, but this type of relationship lacks one crucial component intimacy. Intimacy goes above and beyond sex. Intimacy is allowing the other person to see you for who you really are - no false pretenses, no projected personas, just you. To me, this is true intimacy. Sadly, many relationships today lack such depth. Once upon a time, people actually met someone they liked and went on a date. No, I am not talking about a back and forth WhatsApp conversation. I am talking about a real date. People used to spend time getting to know each other. Who needs to ask someone out on a date when you can just talk to them on Tinder, follow them on Twitter or direct message them on Instagram? I truly believe my generation is guilty of such superficial courtship.

A New Language of Love

Online dating used to be reserved for the older generation. The thirty-somethings were tired of being messed about and wanted to find real love. Online dating used to be about carefully constructing a profile, in order to connect to someone who shared a mutual interest. In this respect, online dating has always been a numbers game. Users sift through date profiles, trying to find someone they are compatible with. Technology is used as a means to get to know the person, in ways that couldn't have been possible through face-to-face interaction. Meeting someone in public is an old-fashioned method. Advocates of online dating find this to be very taxing. For example, you can be attracted to someone you meet in a bar. You then proceed to date this person, which requires a lot of time to truly see if you are compatible. However, the online method allows you to meet many people at once, making it easier to see who you are compatible with. All of this can be done without the need for face-to-face interaction to occur. If and when someone does spark your interest, you can take it one step further, meet offline and go on a date. You are more likely (in theory) to get along with this person as you have spent a lot of time talking to them online.

Throughout the eighteen years I spent in education, I was always told to get the best grades, to acquire the relevant work experience, as all of this would lead to a high paying job. Apart from a few awkward weeks of sex education, love was a topic that was rarely, if ever, discussed. Therefore, it comes as no surprise that many of us are far more career-orientated and focused on success. With our professional development taking prominence, there is arguably insufficient time for a committed relationship. However, this does not mean that we aren't horny creatures that want to have sex whenever possible. The hook-up culture appears to be the perfect solution to the problem. Some of you reading this will argue that people have been having casual sex for decades and yes, that's true. However, the advancements in technology today seem to be facilitating casual sexual encounters in a way that was once impossible. Today, dating apps are molding a new language of love – a language that speaks less about chemistry and more about surface emotions and momentary satisfaction. With over 90 million people using dating apps all around the world, the likelihood of meeting someone is now based on location proximity and how good you look in your profile photo. No wonder many app-initiated dates end up being nothing more than convenient hook ups.

Jdate, Tinder, HitchMe, PlentyofFish, Nervedating, Grindr, Duodater, Happn, DateHookUp, Fellody, eHarmony and Badoo. You name it; there is a dating app for just about anything. If you are a book lover, you can find someone who shares your book tastes on Alikewise. Tastebuds.fm helps you find dates that share your love for music. Lovestruck is a dating app that connects single professionals. There is a dating app for just about every hobby and interest you have. This is all targeted at finding the right person for you… or is it?

Dating apps have become very attractive to the young and single. The primary user base of the infamous dating app Tinder is 18 to 24 years old. We are the dating app generation, craving speed and simplicity when looking for love. Such apps are replacing the traditional core of courtship and leaving an epicenter of multiple temptations and endless possibilities in its wake. Admittedly, I do have a few friends who have found their long-term partners using these apps. However, many more of my peers have used it for sexual liberation. Spoilt for choice, they mine their way through hundreds of profiles, pausing momentarily to swipe. I have never been keen on online dating. However, for the purposes of this book, as well my own curiosity, I signed up to Tinder. The whole process took no more than two minutes. I was impressed by the ease and speed with which I could use the app, and could see why it was so popular. All I had to do was view a few photos and a short paragraph about the Tinder user. Then swipe right if I liked what I saw, if not, left. If the men I liked swiped right too, then we were a match. Simple. After setting my search distance to a 5 mile radius, over 30 males asked me to meet up with them within the first week.

Tinder is like sexting on crack. It facilitates casual hookups in the most efficient way possible. It has proven to be a hit with many young people looking for a good time. This is why some people are becoming disinterested in real-world dating interactions. Being complimented in the street and approached for a number has evolved into a swipe of the thumb and a cheeky one liner targeted at getting the 'draws'. I've asked many of my friends why they use Tinder. Most agreed that it was nothing more than a bit of harmless fun. Whilst others admitted that they had struggled to meet anyone in real life and found the virtual dating world easier to consume. One friend in particular told me that he has approached three girls in person and over 300 online. A few even said that Tinder was something to pass the time. They had no intention of ever meeting anyone they spoke to via the app, they just wanted someone to talk to when they were bored. Nothing more than the modern pen pal.

Are we even looking for anyone in the real world anymore? When I am out with friends, I find that they spend more time looking at their phones, sizing up a person they have found on a dating app. They aren't even remotely interested in the other people at the bar. If we all just looked up for one minute, maybe we would find what we're looking for. I cannot help but feel that we have become more isolated and disconnected. A mere online connection is trivial compared to seeing someone you like in the physical form walking down the street. Dating apps provide immediacy. However, in my opinion, they are diluting the true base of connection and eliminating the significance of face-to-face interactions.

Rejection *(noun)*

the dismissing or refusing of a proposal, idea, etc.
the action of spurning a person's affections.

The Internet seems to be a comfortable place for all aspects of our lives. We have digitised everything from shopping and banking to networking and dating. Perhaps, it is not our fault. We just happened to be growing up when the digital age was in its infancy and have learnt to utilise technology in this way. 'Hooking up' is rather convenient. However, we will never truly be able to love unless we are prepared to liberate ourselves from our own inability to be completely vulnerable. This means connecting with someone on a much deeper level.

If there is one thing I feel my generation fears, it is rejection. Being rejected – irrespective of whether you like the person or not – is always going to be emotionally draining. It is hard to lay our emotions bare for the other person to see. Why? Because in the event that it doesn't work out, we want to be able to soothe our egos with the idea that this person did not get to see all of us. 'Hooking up' without actually connecting and going through the motions of dating, minimises our chances of being hurt. However, it also eliminates the chances of being in a loving relationship.

The Side Chick Test

The Side Chick. Also known as the Mistress, the boo-ty call, the sidepiece, or if you prefer, the side order of rice that comes with your Nando's main. She is a woman who is <u>NOT</u> in a relationship and is having sexual relations with a man who <u>IS</u>. Funnily enough, for a woman who is not that important, she sure has many names. Now that you know who the side chick is, I am going to spend the next few paragraphs ex-plaining her role and responsibilities. You see, some women are actually oblivious to the fact that they are side chicks; they genuinely believe that they are the main chick. I call them the regular side chicks. Bless their hearts, they just don't have a clue. In order to shed some light on the matter, I have devised a test, which will allow some women to gain clarity on their relationship status (or lack thereof). Pay close atten-tion. After reading this, some of you may come to re-alise that you are, in fact, the side chick. I apologise in advance. No, I take that back. Miss Side Chick, you need to know the truth. So here goes...

Note: In order to take this test you will need to answer the questions truthfully, it's for your own good!

- **His House**

Where does he live? You may have a vague idea of the area (if you are lucky) but where does he actually live? Have you ever seen his house, his room or even been on the street he lives on.

• Dating Indoors

Does he opt for a romantic evening indoors, rather than going out on a date because he wants to spend quality time with you? On the rare occasion that he does take you out, does he avoid certain places, keeping the date as low-key as possible.? For example, does he avoid affection, such as holding hands or kissing you in public?

• Social Media Lockdown

Does he claim that he has no interest in Instagram and Twitter or makes excuses as to why your friend request is still pending on Facebook?

• One Call Away

Does he avoid his phone calls when he is with you or makes sure he is out of earshot before answering them?

• Meet and Greet?

Does he distance you from his inner circles? Have you ever met his friends, let alone his parents? Does he avoid double dates and decline invitations to meet your friends? If you do happen to meet someone he knows, it is probably because you bumped into them and he will introduce you as nothing more than a friend.

• Time is of the Essence

Busy, busy, busy. Does he make plans, only to cancel at the last minute? He calls you at random hours of the night. Sometimes he rushes off the phone and says he will call you back and sure enough a couple days later he is asking how you are.

• Physical Attraction

Are all of your 'dates' practically spent in bed? Does he tell you how sexy you are, how he finds you irresistible, nibbles on your ear and then gets you on your back? Think about it!

• What Future?

Does he dismiss any future plans you try and make with him? Constantly changing the subject if you mention a holiday, a weekend break or just an event you want him to attend with you?

End of test.

And the results are in; the scores have been counted and verified...

Dear Miss Side Chick,

If he has never invited you to his house, it is probably because this is where he spends time with his main chick. He does not want you to leave a piece of jewellery behind one day or some hair or any other DNA evidence that will lead to him being caught out. So, he makes sure he comes round to see you instead. Oh, how thoughtful of him. He does not want to be seen with you, that is why he spends so much time indoors, not out for fancy meals in fancy restaurants. If a man is committed to you, he will be happy to have you on his arm, parading you around.

Do not hold your breath for your friend request to be accepted. You will never have the privilege of publicly expressing your 'relationship'. His main chick will be on his social media platforms; there are probably pictures of him and her on his Instagram (the one he claims that he does not have) - the last thing he needs is you uploading a picture of the two of you, or, worse still, a comment on his wall. Social media has become one of the easiest ways to get caught; putting you on social media lockdown will reduce the chances of this. He doesn't like leaving his phone around you just in case the Main calls, remember you are his side chick. You have not met any of his friends or family because that's his main chick's circle. He doesn't want them to know that he is sneaking around with you. The meet and greets are for the main chick only, this does not fall into your duties as a side chick. Fall back! Nobody knows you exist but him and that's just how he wants it to stay.

He cancels plans with you at the last minute because a better offer has probably come up from his main chick. He has invested time and effort into her.

You are not his priority, she is. He is not interested in getting to know you on a deeper level because those moments are reserved for his main squeeze. He is only interested in experiencing you physically, not intellectually.

He does not make any long-term future plans with you because he is making them with her. All he requires from you is a good time, which is why your future goals and aspirations fall on deaf ears. He is taking his Main out on dates, planning holidays and weekends away with her, he is planning on having sex with you and that is just about as far as his future plans go.

Yours Truly,
Fattima Mahdi

So there you have it. There are certain benefits that a main chick has that a side chick will never have. Why? Because they are the side chick. The end. Side chicks are disposable goods. So, naturally, they have an expiration date. Miss Side Chick, do you hear that? *Tick tock tick tock* that is the sound of your time running out. To all the side chicks reading this in disbelief right now, I have a few more things that I want to get off my chest. Stop catching main chick feelings for a man who never wanted you in the first place. Stop devoting your time to someone who is not willing to spend much of their time with you. Stop settling for second place. Stop allowing him to use you. Just stop!

Some side chicks are well aware that they are not the Main and I call them the advanced side chicks. These women are a different species. Yes, there are levels to this. I hope you are keeping up.

The Side Chick Is Evolving

(*Main Chicks Beware*)

Unlike the regular side chick, the advanced side chick is a professional. She knows her role and she plays it well. She does not ask questions such as *"where were you last night?"* and *"why didn't you call me back?"* and she most certainly never has the *"so where is this going?"* talk. She knows that the moment she questions her relationship status or prompts him to make future plans, she will be axed - so the advanced side chick is content. When she is with him, she ensures that he is stress-free. She does not hassle him, give him a headache or expect anything from him. All in all, she makes him feel good. She is planning on moving from his peripheral view, into the central, running the main chick over as she switches lanes. If she plays her cards right, she is well aware that he will end up preferring her to his Main. The advanced side chick is sneaky, she is cunning and ruthless in her approach, and she will steal your man if she is given the opportunity.

"I'd rather b the side chick to a loyal dude...b4 I be the main b**** to a cheater"- Anon

This quote is a caption by a female Instagram user. She is clearly confused. How can a *"dude"* be loyal if he is cheating on his girlfriend with you? It just doesn't make sense. However, I am very glad that she expressed her views. It just goes to show the lame and highly stupid excuses advanced side chicks are prepared to make, so that they can keep fooling around with men who are not theirs. In my opinion, the advanced side chick has very low self-esteem. She needs to feel loved and wanted - and the fact that a taken man is giving her attention only boosts her ego and confidence. It is a sad story.

Main Chick Madness

Ok, enough about the side chicks now; I have probably touched a nerve and lost a few readers. So, to all those who are still with me, it is time to address the main chicks. The women who know that their boyfriend has a side chick but they accept it and say, *"he comes back to me every night"* and *"he loves me, he doesn't love her"*. Now this is something I am really struggling to understand. Your man is cheating on you, to which you are fully aware and you are still with him? Why accept it? How can a man respect you if you do not respect yourself? If it was possible to send slaps through this book, believe me I would!

Maybe even two, just in case the first one didn't register with you. In any case, you are more than welcome to look at the palm of your right hand and slap yourself on my behalf.

If you have successfully transitioned from a former side chick to a main chick and surprise, surprise, you find that your man is now cheating on you with a new side chick - in all honesty you cannot even be mad at him. You should be mad at yourself. Your initial relationship was already based on a lie because he was fooling around with you when he had a girlfriend. Therefore, what makes you think he will be able to resist the temptation from other women now?

Social Media Stalker

There are millions of people online using social networks. Due to the fact that social media has become a significant part of most people's lives; it has also become a significant part of their relationships. Social media is considered a useful tool for communication and constant connection. However, overuse can also be damaging for those in committed relationships. Given the abundance of apps that are readily available for   social interaction, it has grown increasingly difficult for some of us to trust our partners. Hence, why it can be tempting to use social media to scrutinise their online presence. And some of us have gone to great lengths to keep our partners in check. For example, a story was circulating on the Internet about a 17 year-old girl who made a fake Facebook account under the name Chantel. She used this pseudo-profile to send a friend request to her boyfriend – which he accepted. Posing as Chantel, she messaged him and asked if he wanted to meet up with her. Again, he accepted her invitation. Through this honey trap, it became clear that her boyfriend intended to be unfaithful, however, I cannot help but feel that she too was guilty of betrayal. The honey trap was pre-meditated and meticulously planned. She set out to catch him.

I'm not saying any names, but I do know some women who make fake profiles to follow all of their partners' female friends. I kid you not. Instagram, Twitter, Facebook - you name it, they've got it. It can be hard maintaining your own social media outlets, let alone a fake profile. How do they keep up? What normality could there possibly be in their relationship if they have gone to such extremities to keep their man under lock and key? I even have friends who steam over suspicious pictures and comments they come across when thoroughly investigating– sorry, I mean innocently looking at their partner's profile. They'll spend hours building a 'case' against their partner and will often draw elaborate conclusions that are unlikely to be anywhere near the truth. And because they feel both stupid and guilty for cross-examining their partners' online interactions, they can't even ask them about it. If this sounds like you, then this is wholly unhealthy and I urge you to stop. I know it can be easy to get caught up in a social media stalking frenzy. What starts off as a quick browse of their Instagram, can quickly manifest into a fully-fledged project as you analyse their online behaviour and interactions with others. However, if you are taking such drastic precautions, you probably need to re-evaluate why you are with your partner in the first place. Trust is the foundation on which every relationship should be built.

Social media does not single-handedly ruin relationships per se. However, it does pose a threat and it will certainly be used in evidence against you, if you do not mention, when questioned, something that has been found on your Facebook wall, Instagram news feed or Twitter profile. Don't believe me? Tell that to my friend who broke up with his girlfriend because she had not untagged herself from pictures of her ex. It seems childish but it is a growing problem in the modern relationship, which is putting a strain on the longevity of them.

If you are being followed by too many random people on your social networks this is sure to raise a few eyebrows, if you happen to like that model's photo, be prepared for the backlash, and if you do not want to appear *In A Relationship* on Facebook, you better have a damn good reason why. An *In a Relationship* status online is akin to a wedding ring for some people. Declaring your love to all your 1,756 friends, (half of whom you've never met or don't even speak to?), it couldn't get any more official than that. There are so many more demands on a modern relationship that simply saying *"I love you"* is no longer enough. Now you have to plaster it on all your social media handles with 'original' captions, such as *#mygirlisbetterthanyourgirl*. Why wouldn't you want to display this information online? What are you hiding? Well, perhaps you just do not want other people to be in your business but relay this to your partner. Otherwise, they may start to wonder how much you actually value your relationship.

"Last Seen"

Instant messaging services such as WhatsApp are great for communicating in real time. The app is loaded with features, one of which is the *Last Seen* timestamp. When enabled, this feature allows you to see the exact time that one of your contacts was last active online. Another feature is the *Message info* screen, this allows you to see when your message has been successfully delivered to the recipient, as well as the exact time the message was read. These two features in particular, make for a deadly combo, causing a lot of drama in relationships. When sending a message on WhatsApp, many people expect an immediate reply. Especially if it's clear that the recipient is online and has already read the message. This expectation is amplified when the recipient happens to be their boyfriend or girlfriend.

A friend of mine would frequently message her boyfriend and he would always be slow to reply. When she queried him about it, he said it was because he was busy. However, she pointed out that the *"Last Seen"* timestamp showed that he was active online hours after he had read her message. She grew very frustrated with him and suspected foul play. In the hopes that it would put her mind at ease, he sent her screenshots of the people he was talking to at specific times on the app. I am sure many of you are familiar with this scenario. Whether or not you have been the one analysing timestamps or pleading your innocence, it has probably driven some, if not all of you, crazy.

Regardless of whether you want to spy on your partner or not, WhatsApp features make it easy to keep tabs on them. I remember waking up one morning at university (I was 19 years old) and seeing that my then boyfriend had been active on WhatsApp at 4am. I immediately asked him who he had been talking to at that early hour. Needless to say he was offended at what I was insinuating. Not too long after that, I disabled the *Last Seen* timestamp. I did not want to be the girlfriend who nitpicked at everything he did, nor did I want to drive myself insane every time he was active online. WhatsApp can cause so much unnecessary drama. At face value, it can appear that your boyfriend or girlfriend is ignoring you and prioritising someone else. In actuality, this could all be harmless and they may just not be in a position to give you their full attention.

The 'Perfect' Couple

We all know a couple that document their highly cu-rated snapshot lives all over our Facebook news feeds. They make their relationship seem so effort-less, accumulating hundreds of *Likes* and *Comments* such as "*aww, this is so sweet*", "*#RelationshipGoals*" and so on and so forth. They are the couple that many of us secretly try and emulate. Or, if you are a hater - then you secretly pray for their demise, be-cause they are just so happy and in love, and you envy that. Be warned. Every relationship has its problems. Social media allows us to showcase the best, or what appears to be the best of our relation-ship for the public eye to melt over. Nobody is per-fect. No, not even Melissa and Shaun who have been together for five years and constantly upload Selfies where they are smooching every other minute.

#NotAnotherUpdate

For many people I know, social media is an extension of the self. It may as well be a phantom limb as they cannot go more than a few minutes without scrolling through various social channels and updating their various profiles. It seems to me that they value their virtual lives over their real lives. Every trip to a res-taurant must be documented on Instagram with "*#foodporn*" and every time they are out with their partner they must let the online world know in real time. *"Chilling with bae… off to the shops with bae… about to go cinema with bae… at the cinema with bae".* Why do some people think it's necessary to constantly update every single thing they are doing with their partner? Yes, I understand that you want to parade your relationship because you are proud of it and whatnot. But are you in a relationship or are you and your Twitter followers and Facebook friends in a relationship? There's a difference between building memories of your previous experiences with your partner and posting up a status every time you are with them. How can you enjoy the moment with your partner if you are too busy trying to take the best Selfie to post on Instagram? By allowing unparalleled access into your relationship, you give all of your friends the go ahead to be nosy and add their two pence in whenever they feel like it. You are the one who is going to feel uncomfortable when your friend starts telling you that they read a suspicious *Comment* your partner posted on someone's Facebook wall or *Liked* a suggestive picture on Instagram.

Distracted

Preoccupation with social media is not just limited to over-sharing your relationship online; it can also serve as a substitute for physical presence and real world interactions with your partner. For example, I was once sat in a restaurant enjoying a catch-up with a close friend. A couple walked in and was seated next to us. The male spent the whole time with his head in his phone, only looking up to engage with the waiter and make an order. I couldn't help but feel sorry for his female counterpart who spent half of her time staring into space and the other half trying desperately to get his attention, all the while looking uncomfortable with the whole situation. So much energy and time is spent keeping up appearances in the online world, that the quality time spent as a couple can be degraded. It really is a modern struggle.

8. Code Red

We are animals. We may be socialised and well-trained animals with morals and principals, but we are still animals. Monogamy is a social construct. We have been taught to engage in one-to-one relationships, but this isn't always easy. What is cheating? Some people argue that flirting is harmless and kissing someone else is trivial. Perceptions of what constitutes as cheating are not uniform. It's all relative. The boundaries you set for yourself and the boundaries your partner has set for you (and vice versa) are likely to differ in some ways. Some couples assume that they don't need to define what cheating means to them. They think that their partner will naturally share the same opinion. And this, ladies and gentleman, is how problems arise. People have claimed to be wholly unaware that they were in fact cheating because, in their eyes, it did not meet their definition. So what's your definition? If you're not quite sure where you stand on the matter, simply picture your partner kissing, touching or slow grinding with someone else and decide whether or not it would upset you. If it would then yep, you guessed right, it's cheating. One of my male friends told me that he doesn't consider oral sex to be cheating. When I asked him if he would allow another man to perform such an act on his girlfriend, he quickly changed his mind. In my opinion, any degree of sexual intimacy is cheating. If you truly love your partner, don't hurt them.

Liked!

The Internet has created many detached relationships. Therefore, it is understandable that people would view acts carried out online in a different light to those of the real world. However, it is important to realise that what you do online can have implications offline too. Many of us spend numerous hours of the day with our noses in our phones, browsing the Internet. Apps like Instagram create a fantasy world for many men and women. There are a variety of filters that can be applied to images. Choosing the right one can be an agonising decision. The applied filters and other photo-editing mobile apps leave many uploads portraying ideals rather than real people.

A lot of my male friends who are in a relationship have admitted to following women who take provocative pictures on Instagram. When I asked why they felt the need to scroll through these seductive profiles, they said it was harmless. I beg to differ. In some ways online interactions that are motivated by sexual interest could be seen as cheating. Fellas, if you feel the need to lust over another woman's picture online then you are clearly not satisfied with your partner. You wouldn't walk up to a scantily clad female on the street and tell them that you like them. So why it is ok to *Like* a provocative picture on Instagram? A *Like* is a compliment and you are complimenting someone by engaging with his or her images in this way.

An Emotional Affair

You treat this particular person as a confidant and share secrets that you would not even share with your partner. Though there are no physical boundaries being broken, you've still developed a strong and intense connection with this person. You are emotionally invested. You know that what you feel for this person is deeper than a friendship because you want to look your best when you are around them. You dress up for this person and find excuses to meet up with them, even if it means cancelling plans with your partner. Why? Because all you want to do is be with them. You may not even have kissed this person, let alone had sex with them. But, emotionally, you have cheated. This, in some ways, is actually worse than committing the physical act. Relationships are more than the physical; emotionally you have to give yourself to your partner. You have to share all of you; mind and body.

A friend of mine found a string of private messages between her partner and another woman on Facebook. Though there was no indication of them meeting up, the content was suggestive and my friend considered this to be a level of cheating. At first, I thought she was overreacting, but then I sat down and had a long think about it. Talking to someone online every day requires a level of intimacy. The personal nature of the conversation in itself is a telltale sign that you are seeking a deeper connection from someone other than your partner. There is a thin line between innocent flirting and flirting with intent. Once those lines become blurred, it can cause major problems. You may not be physically cheating but when something of significance happens and the first person you want to tell is the person you have been flirting with online, then you are emotionally investing yourself in someone other than your partner.

Why Do People Cheat?

People are often unfaithful when they do not feel valued and respected by their primary partner. Everyone wishes to feel significant and cherished, especially from the most important person in their life. When people feel that they are being taken for granted or are being used for convenience, they are likely to find someone else who will give them the attention they deserve. Think about it. If you have spent the whole day with your partner and then someone makes a move on you that evening, you will probably shrug them off. Whereas, if you haven't seen your partner for a while and someone else is making you feel loved by simple flattery and flirtatious acts, then the likelihood of you cheating may increase somewhat. Ask yourself this question - is cheating really worth it? All you are doing is experiencing an orgasm with someone else. Is an orgasm really worth sacrificing all the love you share with your partner? If the answer is yes, then maybe you're not in a worthy relationship.

It is easier to refrain from actively coming on to someone. But what do you do if the script is flipped and someone comes on to you? Simple. You make sure that under no circumstances are you ever able to get into a situation where you can cheat. I repeat, make sure that under no circumstances are you ever able to get into a situation where you can cheat.

I Must Confess

The deed is done. You have cheated. Now what? Some of you will have no problem keeping this dirty secret. After all, it is only going to hurt them, so it would be selfish of you to tell them what you have done, right? Telling your partner is allowing them to choose whether or not they still want to pursue the relationship. Not telling your partner is YOU making a choice for them and that is unacceptable. As hard as it may be, and as much as you are worried that you will lose them, you cheated. Now you have to deal with the consequences.

Once a Cheat...

There's nothing worse than finding out that the person you love(d) has cheated you. Once a cheat... always a cheat? This may not be the case. It is up to you to decide what happens next. Sometimes, we want our friends to talk us into making a tough decision, so that we don't have to. Pay less attention to what your friends say. They will naturally want to fight your corner and they will do their best to support you, even if it means suggestions such as keying cars, throwing bricks at windows or cutting up clothes. Remember to handle the situation rationally and in a mature manner. Take some time to outline your position and thoroughly evaluate how you should proceed. I mentioned earlier that what constitutes as cheating can be defined in various ways, so the decision you make will be dependent on what your definition is. Personally, I have a zero-tolerance policy for cheating. I know that I will not be able to trust him again and a relationship void of trust is not worth being in. However, my friend's current boyfriend cheated on her in the past. They separated for some time but now they are back together and their relationship is stronger than ever.

9. Worth The Fight?

Every couple has arguments. Personally, I do not think arguing is a bad thing at all. You and your partner are not going to agree on everything and arguing allows you to iron out any discrepancies that you may have. In fact if you and your partner never argue, this could be a sign that you are keeping things bottled up - rather than thinking the relationship is strong enough to work through them.

In some instances, the genesis of an argument is less to do with the issue at hand and more to do with the many things that have gone unsaid throughout your relationship. For example, your partner's bad habits. At first you didn't think they were worth confronting, so you left them unchecked. Now they've compounded and become a much bigger problem and as a result, little things he or she does, irritate you far beyond the norm. For example, they've arrived ten minutes late. They have a perfectly good excuse – they were stuck in traffic. Rather than give them the benefit of the doubt and assume it was out of their control, you initiate a full-blown argument.

"you should've known it was rush hour… why didn't you message me?" If they had been late on many occasions, you're outburst would've been justified. However, this was a one off. If you were in a good place with your partner and there weren't any underlying problems affecting your mood, you probably would have let it go. After all, they were only ten minutes late.

- **The Wall**

You are angry. You have so much you want to get off your chest and it's all falling on deaf ears. Your attempts to communicate are being dismissed. Sure, they are pretending to listen and take your opinion on board, but you know deep down that they are no longer paying attention. You can barely get anything more than an *"ok"* out of them.

- **The War**

You are going toe for toe, round for round, screaming back and forth and trying to assert your authority over one another. They are not listening to you. You are certainly not listening to them. You are right, you know you are right and they are wrong. Full stop!

Both types of arguments are equally frustrating. If you cannot swallow your pride and admit to your faults, then how can your relationship work? Constantly being defensive and assuming that everything is their fault will not get you anywhere. Some people say all they need to say in an argument and then walk away. This leaves the other person feeling frustrated because they were unable to vent. They may even feel guilty over the other leaving. When he or she does return, they do not want to continue the argument and so they are never given the chance to get their point across. It is frustrating for that person to bear the burden of being the 'problem'. Running away from every argument, leaves unresolved issues to fester and will slowly but surely eat away at your relationship. If you want it to work, you are going to have to put your heads together to find a solution.

The conflict has long since passed but the issue hasn't really been resolved. Quite frankly, you're both still pissed off. The residue of your argument has left you both wanting to get back at each other. You know what I'm talking about. You're going out more than usual, flirting with your friends and they are doing the same. It seems harmless, but is it? Every action sparks a reaction and it can become quite heated, especially when you are both trying to 'win'. Be careful! Behaving in such a way can lead to a break up that neither of you actually wanted.

Some people use an argument to manipulate and demean each other, or worse still; they throw ultimatums around – *"well, maybe we should just end it".* Those of you, who are quick to render the relationship irreparable rather than seeking a resolution, are not affording your relationship the respect it deserves. All you want is for him to say sorry, you want her to listen to you and you hope the ultimatum will make them realise that you cannot be taken for granted. Ultimatums are not a viable solution to re-solving the problem at hand. Even when you finally mean it (this time), your request will not be taken seriously because you have said it countless times in the past, and nothing has come of it.

When you are angry, your ability to make ra-tional decisions is compromised. Heated arguments can sometimes lead to you saying something that cannot be forgiven. Emotions affect everything - calm down, sleep on it and see how you feel in the morn-ing. I have seen too many relationships go down the drain, due to a quick and sharp tongue, which fails to stifle its uncalculated utterances. When it is all said and done, you cannot take it back and depending on the severity of your words - it might lead to the ab-rupt and painful ending of your relationship.

"I Think We Should Take A Break"

After a big fight there are many different ways peo-ple choose to solve their argument. Some have make-up sex, some seek advice from family and friends and some will try to negotiate in order to reach a com-mon ground. Others will become stubborn, failing to mention the issue again. Some couples take a break. I have touched on the struggles people face when try-ing to get into a serious relationship. However, that is nothing compared to the issues people face once in the relationship. Major problems can arise if there is a constant switch from being 'on' one minute and 'off' the next. For one, you'll be putting the longevity of your relationship in jeopardy. How can you develop a strong and healthy union if you often break up to make up? Secondly, if you're not careful, a break could also lead to unwelcomed infidelity as new relationships are formed while you're 'off' with your partner. It's a cycle. Make up your mind. You either have to be all in or all out, or at least shed some clarity on what is actually going on. If you're taking a break every five minutes, then you clearly do not feel that the relationship is worth fixing. Instead, you are just running away from the recurring problem.

Addressing the Problem

People take breaks in order to redefine relationships. How do you want yours to be redefined? Has this been outlined? What are the rules of the break? Are you both aware? For example, are you allowed to sleep with other people? Are you allowed to talk to each other? Or are you completely cutting ties with one another for a set period of time? How will you know when the break ends? If you do not know the answers to these questions and you are currently on a break, then you need to think long and hard about where you stand. Without proper understanding, taking a break is like going on holiday. It is an opportunity to explore new sights, new people and have wild adventures. But just like any holiday, there comes a time when you have to return home and re-sume normal life. In this case, this means your rela-tionship. In the event that you and your partner are still having problems, you may decide to take more breaks. After all, there is the added assurance that you will be able to come home whenever you want and re-enter the relationship. So what are you taking a break from? If your partner feels like they need more space or keeps talking to their ex, then he or she needs to go on a break. They need to work on these issues with the eventuality of correcting it be-fore you can resume your relationship. Otherwise, you will still end up with the same age-old issues you had before you went on the break in the first place.

Too Broke to Fix

The honeymoon stage can last anywhere between a few weeks and a few months. If you're really lucky, maybe even a year. Throughout this period you feel very connected to your partner, you enjoy the same things, spend a lot of time together and you couldn't be hap-pier. Once this phase wears off, the real test in the relationship begins. The negative traits that your partner has always possessed are now at the forefront and have a greater impact on your percep-tion of them. In addition, you and your partner may feel like you are losing the connection you initially had, becoming preoccupied with hobbies and spend-ing a lot less time together. Every relationship goes through this phase and it is a necessary evil. If you make it through this intermittent period of falling out of love to fall back in love, then your relationship will mature. Sadly, not every relationship is sustainable and it can be unhealthy for you to make excuses that mask this fact. After countless compromises, there comes a time when you need to assess the current climate in which you find yourself and determine whether or not the relationship is a fruitless endeavour. When you have been in a long-term relationship, it is easy to get comfortable. All the signs are there that the relationship has eroded but you just can't seem to leave. For example, neither of you feel the same way about each other, and you are both very unhappy. You have grown apart, changed and evolved. Yet, somehow you ignore this and it can happen for a number of reasons.

• I Don't Want To Be Alone

You might be afraid of being alone. It can be difficult to revert back to being a single entity because you are so used to being with your partner.

• I Don't Want To Look Like A Failure

You do not want to look like a failure. Your peers and family members have become acquainted with your partner. They have welcomed them into the family and constantly congratulate you on your relationship. Not to mention that your future has already been outlined - marriage, baby names and the like.

You are always going to disappoint someone, even if you are doing everything right. It is important to remain conscious of the fact that you don't need a partner to validate you. In fact, it is refreshing when I see my friends make the conscious, yet tough decision, to walk away from something that is wasting time, instead of adhering to other people's expectations.

• I Want Them To Break Up With Me

You are waiting for your partner to break up with you. You know that you don't want to be with them but you'd rather not hurt their feelings. So, instead of breaking up with them, you try and sabotage the relationship. You may become distant in the hopes they will break up with you. Tut. Tut. Tut. Once you know that you don't want to be with your partner, you owe it to them to make your feelings known. Breaking up with someone is a hard thing to do. Making it look like it was your partner's decision, so that you can be exempt from doing it yourself is cowardly.

• I Have Invested Too Much Time

If you remain in a relationship solely because you believe that you have invested too much time in your partner, you really are selling yourself short. Some people are reluctant to break up because they do not want someone else to benefit from all the hard work they have put in. Would you rather forgo your happiness to ensure that another person cannot be in a happy relationship with your partner? For every minute you spend as a self-proclaimed coach, clutching the man or woman you have 'trained' up so well, you are wasting your time and delaying your destiny.

- ### What If I Don't Find Anyone Else?

You shouldn't remain in a relationship solely because you're worried that you'll look back on an eternity of failed relationships and wonder if they were, in fact 'the one'. If you know that your relationship has run its course, you're going to have to suck it up and move on.

10. The Aftermath

We always seem to give the 'best' advice when our friends are going through problems in their relationship. We find it easy to say what they should and shouldn't do and this is often because we will not be the ones directly affected by it. However, as soon as we are faced with the same difficult situation, our opinions change. Needless to say, being emotionally involved can restrict your ability to make optimal decisions. If you've gone through a series of rough patches with your partner, you may need to look at what has gone wrong from an objective standpoint. It's not until you are on the outside looking in that you can wholly understand how naive you were and how much pain you went through just to realise it.

Why Do We Break Up?

We break up with people who are bad communicators, people who bore us, as well as people we feel are restricting us from reaching our potential. We also break up with people who are emotionally unavailable, irresponsible or lazy. Sometimes we get caught up. We know the relationship is in free-fall and will probably hit the ground at any given moment. Nevertheless, we 'soldier' on, kind of like that job we hate so much. Until years pass, we've had enough of all the bull and finally pluck up the courage to leave. The time between knowing we need to break up and actually breaking up can vary. I know friends who have stayed in a relationship a year or two longer than necessary. There seemed to be a lag between the realisation that their relationship was failing and the actual break up.

The Good News About Bad Breakups

Have you ever felt like you have given someone everything, only to be betrayed? Perhaps this left you reluctant to enter a new relationship for fear of being hurt again. I get it. You are emotionally concerned about making new connections. As a result, you've now set the bar very high so that no one will ever be able to measure up to your standards. No one likes to be hurt, especially when many sacrifices have been made and sufficient time has been invested. Before you enter into a new relationship, you should first acknowledge what happened, why it happened and give yourself sufficient time to fully recover from the break up. That age old saying 'what doesn't kill you makes you stronger' could never be truer. If you let a bad relationship define you, then it will define you. It is that simple.

So, what is the good news about bad breakups? Well, first of all, (in theory) a break up will allow you to gain a better understanding of yourself. If there was a bad habit you exhibited whilst in the relationship, assess it and decide whether this is something you want to omit before proceeding into a new relationship. Are you the common denominator? Ladies, if you find yourself dating a series of guys that have gone on to cheat, then you need to stop and think about what it is that attracts you to these types of men. Otherwise, the cycle will continue to repeat itself, over and over and over again. Fellas, if you have been with a string of women who lack substance and would rather keep up with the Kardashians than have a thought provoking conversation with you, then you need to question why you attract these types of women.

If you fail to notice your own shortcomings and exaggerate the role that your ex played in the termination of the relationship, then you will struggle to gain anything positive from the break up, and you are more likely to make the same mistakes going forward. Therefore, it is important that you use this time to reflect on what went wrong and use this new experience as a new lesson.

Rebounds and Rewinds

In a desperate attempt to move on from a break up, some of us quickly enter new relationships. However, this is merely a physical attachment we form with someone else, in the hope that it will mentally free us of the person we shared so much with. We think that if we are able to love someone else then we will be free from the pain. Rebounds are a way to dismiss the reality that you have broken up with someone you liked or loved very much. You will find reasons as to why your new partner is more compatible and draw comparisons between them and your ex. This relationship will never go anywhere because you have not given yourself the time to get over the past. If you find yourself sleeping with your ex every now and then, you are definitely not over it yet. Why? Because you still long for the intimacy, even though you know it was the right decision to break up with them in the first place. So, you and your ex have been apart for about three months now. Every now and then they message you to see how you have been and you find yourself thinking about them for the remainder of the day. Sometimes they come round to your house and you cannot resist the temptation to have sex. Though you are no longer in a relationship, you cannot help but maintain the intimate bond you share. Meanwhile, they are still exercising their single rights and dating other people... or worse. In your mind, you are still with your ex, but in theirs, you are certainly not together. How can you move forward if you keep looking back? Your ex keeps saying that you might get back together in the future, but why not now? What are they waiting for? Well, maybe they are stalling to see if a better option comes up. Do not be a contingency plan or an insurance policy, in case their next relationship doesn't work.

Should I Get Back With My Ex?

Your ex could be sabotaging your future because they cannot let go. You know, that ex who randomly pops up to get an update on your life and wants to know if you're still single, so that they can seize the opportunity to pounce. Or, the ex who entered into a new relationship and has since realised that you are actually perfect for them. They know they messed up and now they want you back. If you were the one who initiated the break up, then your ex might not understand why you no longer want to be with them. They might tell you how much they miss you and need you in their life. Stay strong. If you know that they didn't treat you well - perhaps they used you, was controlling or disrespectful - then you shouldn't get back with them. If you did, you would be re-entering the same malfunctioning relationship you managed to break away from. Be happy that you got out of it when you did and do not go back down the road to unhappiness.

Perhaps you're finding that single life is quite lonely and you would rather be with your ex than be by yourself. I have said it before and I will say it again, there is nothing wrong with being single. You do not need a partner to validate you, and although it can be hard to adapt after being in a relationship, trust me, you will cope.

Getting Over It

Breaking up with your partner is hard enough; never mind having to actually deal with your emotions after the fact. A lot of people fool themselves into thinking that they are over it and they have moved on. However, the reality is that they most certainly still have feelings for that person. In some instances, they even end up dating someone who looks just like their previous partner... awkward!

With all the social media outlets that are easily accessible, it does not help that your ex is now one click away. If you find yourself on their Facebook page, scrolling through their recent uploads, status updates, as well as places they have been, then you are most certainly still interested in your ex's life. Which means there is something still there. If you are still hanging on to the memories (i.e. there are still pictures of you two on your phone, on your Facebook wall, Instagram and in your house) then these are telltale signs that you are not yet over it. If you decided to make your relationship public on Facebook and refuse to change your relationship status to single for fear of everyone knowing, then guess what, you are still not over it yet. If you are still focusing on why you broke up in the first place, reliving everything that was said and thinking about what could have been done differently, then you are not over it. As long as you still think that there is hope of getting back together, yep, you guessed right again... you are just not over it.

If you really want to get over your ex and move on with your life, you will need to stop talking to them and stop talking about them. Stop asking them about their day all the time, stop asking mutual friends if they've seen your ex with someone else, and stop scrolling through their socials and spying on what they have been up to. I have done this with an ex of mine, it was difficult to cut the ties but I felt much better afterwards. I stopped enquiring about him and I started focusing on me. And you can too. So change the channel and find something new to shout about.

Friends With An Ex?

Can you be friends with an ex? Well, I have tried that and it certainly did not work for me. Maintaining that connection with someone you have been intimate with will greatly reduce your chances of recovering from the break up. The real test of this friendship is when one, or both of you, find a new partner. It's important to note that, albeit non-intimate, you and your ex are still intertwined in a relationship. If they happen to find a new boyfriend or girlfriend, just how long do you think your friendship will last? You two were getting on so well as friends and you thought there was a chance that you would get back together. Now you have been replaced, all of your hopes and dreams have been crushed and you're wondering whether or not breaking up was the right thing to do in the first place. But it's too late; they have moved on. Now you're left in a state and it feels much worse than you're initial break up.

The Hard Part

When you get wind of the news that your ex has found someone new, it can conjure up many different emotions - sadness, rejection, anxiety and so on. We have all been there. It hurts. In fact, it burns. There's no point in trying to fight these emotions, it's a normal part of the healing process, and it will get easier with time. Do not source out your ex's new girlfriend or boyfriend's Facebook profile and other social media accounts. You will torture yourself if you keep checking up on what they have been up to. So refrain from this at all costs. It can be very tempting to have a quick browse through their profile. However, this might turn into constant checkups, once a week or even once a day. It is irrelevant - focus on you, go out with friends, do something that makes you happy.

Bouncing Back

When you're the one who's decided to break up, you'll find that the healing process isn't really that bad. However, if you happen to be on the receiving end of a break up, it can be quite stressful. Firstly, your ego will suffer a major blow. You may question certain aspects of your personality and see these as reasons for the break up. Take some time to consider why your relationship failed. What went wrong? What will you do differently? What will you expect from your partner in your new relationship? Are there any new deal breakers? Remember, there is a difference between assessing your previous relationship and remaining stagnant in your thoughts. Reflect on your relationship. Do not live in it.

You have gone from being a *we* to an *I* and from an *us* to a *me*. At first, it can be hard but in time you'll enjoy being single. I know I have said this before and I'm going to keep on saying it, time and time again. You do not need to be in a relationship to feel validated. Being single allows you to get to know yourself better, experience new things and enjoy your hobbies and interests. You have a lot more free time now, so use it. Do not rush into anything new; take it slow and meet new people when you feel you are ready.

Blank Slate

After a break up, the healing process begins and in time, you are able to express feelings for someone else. Now that you are in a new relationship, there may be certain aspects of your new partner that you wish were more like your ex. There may also be specific things that you like about your new relationship, which both outline and justify the reasons why you are no longer with your ex. Perhaps your ex didn't pay you enough attention or was never spontaneous. Your new partner does all these things and more. But something is missing. Deep down, you wish your ex possessed these qualities because they are the one you really want to be with. Do not get so caught up in the past that you compromise your future. A blank slate is the always the best way to proceed. We naturally want to compare but no two people are the same.

When an ex has hurt you, it can really sting, leaving you in fear of being vulnerable again. If your last boyfriend or girlfriend cheated on you, you may assume that your current partner will do the same. This is not a good way to enter a new relationship. Your current partner is not to blame for your ex's mistakes. You will only put strain on the relationship if your partner has to bear the weight of something they had no control over. I had a friend who found out that his girlfriend cheated on him and he has not been the same since. He does not treat women with the respect they deserve and I think this is unfair. He is punishing everyone for something that happened to him a long time ago and has allowed his ex to spoil him for someone else. Do not be damaged goods. Love requires you to take the plunge and give it your all. If you want to form healthy romantic relationships, you need to learn to be vulnerable again. Shutting down may seem like the best option but it's not. We naturally emulate preventive measures that others have taken in order to protect ourselves. If you withdraw your emotions from a relationship, your partner is likely to do the same. You know when you see someone running and have no idea why, but you start running with them in order to avoid the unknown danger you assume there is? Well, that is what emotional unavailability is like. If you do not want to be open, then they will not feel comfortable being open either. Once upon a time, I didn't want to put my feelings on the table. I kept my guard up and made it difficult for my boyfriend to connect with me on a much deeper level, often shying away from certain topics of conversation. Expressing my feelings meant that I was giving him a part of me. I have matured over the years and have learned a lot about myself, which has allowed me to correct this problem. As hard as it may be, it is important that you give your new partner the opportunity to make you happy.

11. To Be Loved

Antony was a smooth operator; he knew what to say and when to say it. I had only known him for a brief period (twelve days to be exact) and he was already buying me gifts and confessing his 'love' for me. The icing on the cake was when he bought me a present on his birthday and said, *"My birthday is your birthday"*. This was all too much for me to take in - our romantic relationship was non-existent and our friendship was premature. I could not help but think that there was something else causing him to behave in such an irrational way. He seemed to be more in love with the idea of love. The fantasy. I could not even meet him one-eighth of the way, let alone half, so I was forced to wave my red flag. If someone I barely know can profess such strong feelings for me so soon, then how long until they lose interest and fall 'in love' with someone else just as quickly? If I was the kind of woman who believed in fairytales, then I am sure his sugar-coated utterances would have left me all gooey and warm inside, like the core of a chocolate brownie. Hell, some of my friends were even cooing over his romantic acts and telling me that if I wasn't interested, they definitely were. He was that good! I will never really know if his intentions were genuine. What I do know is that love at first sight just does not exist in my vocabulary, so I am not prepared to build a relationship based on such a fallacy.

There's No Rush

Dating someone new tends to be accompanied by excitement. Once we get to know our partners, we often think about how they will fit into our lives and if our family members and peers will like them. Thinking about the future is not a bad thing. After all, it is always good to get a sense of the direction that the relationship may take. However, when you think about the future too much (so much so that the present hasn't even had an opportunity to run its course), it can put pressure on a relationship. Especially when that relationship is still in the embryonic stages. The one thing that is constant is change. Your partner may change, you may change - who knows, you may even change together, but at least wait until you have known each other more than ten minutes before sending out wedding invitations. Rushing to make a commitment with someone you barely know can lead to bitter disappointment. You may think you know and love this person but that doesn't necessarily mean it's true. Who you think is a Mr. or Mrs. Right could easily be a Mr. or Mrs. Right Now. It will take you longer than a few weeks to differentiate between the two.

A committed relationship is essentially a mini-marriage. Some people rush into a relationship and then start complaining about the headache it is causing once the honeymoon period is over. The first few months were great, but now you realise that this is not the person you want to spend the rest of your life with. You thought they were perfect, but now you know that they burp every five minutes, they want five children, but you only want one and they want to move to Italy, whereas you have no intentions of ever relocating. Do not confuse novelty with feelings. The persona we project when we enter into a new relationship is not often a true representation of who we are. Essentially, we are on our best behaviour, wanting to impress our new lover. It is only after some time that the bad habits start to shine through and that is when our partner gets to see all sides of us and vice versa. I had a friend who invested so much time into her new relationship that she ended up moving in with him after three weeks. Soon after, she regretted her decision. To make matters worse, she was in denial about what she thought was 'true love'. She had sacrificed so much to be with him and felt that she must (and I quote) *"see it through to the end"*. If there ever comes a time when you look at your relationship as a task that you feel obligated to see through, then this is a sure-fire sign that it is time to call it a day. Anyway, after four months of deliberation, she finally plucked up the courage to end it.

She has since entered a new relationship, which she has decided to take slow. Some things can't be rushed. Before you go declaring your love and falling head over heels for a man or woman you barely know, stop and think. Do they know your most annoying habits and flaws? Do you know theirs? We all want the perfect relationship but no one is perfect. It is about accepting them for who they are - flaws and all. This usually takes... time.

Three Little Words

Relationships are built on milestones. You start by dating, if everything is going well then you go over that first hurdle and make it official. If you happen to make it a little further down the line in your relationship, you'll meet close friends and parents. Somewhere, amidst of all this, comes those three little words...

I love you.

This is either welcomed with joy and happiness or an awkward uncomfortable silence in which a hell of a lot of tumbleweed rolls by. Saying these words is essentially a declaration of how you feel and more importantly, what your partner means to you. So, how does saying "*I love you*" change the course of your relationship? Some people say it in a sexually charged situation and use it to manipulate the other to get what they want. Some women think it is a man's job to confess and utter it first, whilst some men think that women should be the one to say it first. Once you say it, there is no going back; your cards are on the table. Your partner can either decide to play their hand or choose to fold. I guess it all depends on how the cards have been dealt. Remember, you are expressing how YOU feel, so you should not dictate, nor expect an immediate response from them. After saying "*I love you*" some are quick to apologise. They may even use disclaimers such as *"I know I'm moving too fast"* or *"it's ok if you don't feel the same",* to fill the silence. These people are responding on behalf of their partner, rather than giving them the option to do so. If the shoe is on the other foot and you are not ready to hear it, do you say "*I love you*" back, solely to make them feel better? I know it feels like you have been put on the spot (and I guess in some ways you have). However, you are under no obligation to reciprocate if you do not feel the same. Three little words. Say it too soon and this could send your relationship hurtling towards impending doom, but wait too long and it may lead to quiet animosity.

Open Up

The internet has brightened our eyes and widened our scope. We want more, seek more and often get more. From the rise of feminism, to gay rights, it's clear that our society is changing, being molded by those challenging the status quo. There has been a conscious shift in how we perceive relationships. Who said that two men can't be in love? Who said that we can't be gender-fluid? Who said that men and women have to get married? Many of us are abandoning the age-old courtship methods and opting for more efficient and tailored ways of finding love. The preset model for love is a one-size-fits-all approach to relationships, where two people meet, fall madly in love, get married and bear children. However, it is estimated that just over half of all marriages end in divorce, so, to some extent, this model is flawed. Monogamy is a social construct and it hasn't worked for everyone. Some people may feel trapped and dissatisfied with their partner, but they may also feel obligated to remain in their relationship, as a result, they end up seeking gratification elsewhere. Perhaps, if we let go of our commitment to a sole being, we would be happier and more fulfilled in our relationships.

Polyamory challenges everything we know about romantic relationships. It means that we can be open in our approach to love and can be intimate with multiple partners at the same time. Polyamorous relationships allow us to explore our feelings without fear or guilt. They are based on honest communication, with full consent given from all parties involved. Stripped of traditional norms and values, being open means that people can customise their relationship in a way that works for them. Setting your own boundaries sounds like a breath of fresh air, it's innovative in nature and seeks to solve the issues relating to ownership and being unfaithful. However, it's an approach to partnership that I find daunting. The concept of loving more than one person, of being intimate with multiple people, is too much, at least, for me to bear.

Many of us are looking forward and letting go of the standards that were set by previous generations. We watched their relationships fail and want better for ourselves. It's clear we aren't naturally monogamous and in response, we appear to be creating a world where we can freely love more people. A world where we don't own one another but rather loan one another. Where we don't cheat, we speak. We remain faithful to our partner by simply being honest with our feelings.

12. Conclusion

Love. Many of you will have your own idea of what love is. This perhaps derives from the love you have witnessed between members of your family, friends and, of course, what you yourself have felt. We have all experienced it in one way or another but what exactly is it? We created it, constructing a four-letter word to explain how we feel. In a sense, it only exists because we say it does. Therefore, it's important to think about whether or not we would still know what love is if it had no definition. I think it's safe to say that love is a beautiful thing. However, what happens when the romantic films we watch distort reality, making us believe in fairytale endings that are impossible to achieve? After all, they were founded on idealistic constructions of what love 'ought' to be. Hollywood's depiction of what it means to be in love is often far-fetched, but they do a very good job of getting you to buy into their elaborated and somewhat eccentric versions of romance. Years and years of regurgitated movie plots have done a good job of making us believe that 'the one' exists.

We see so many 'perfect' relationship portrayals on-screen and then use this as a marker for what love should be. But there is no uniform definition.

Love is a choice. Love is not tangible. You can't just pick it up and put it in your pocket. You can't just stumble upon love on a late Friday afternoon while navigating your way through the hustle and bustle of the commuters on their way home from work. Love stems from an accumulation of emotions and feelings that we attribute to the ones we care about. Love is what you make it. It's not always going to be an easy ride and there will always be ups and downs. Love is swallowing your pride. Love is saying that you are sorry. Love is about compromise, being thoughtful, selfless (sometimes) and so much more. There will always be pitfalls in a relationship. Arguments over delayed WhatsApp responses or concerns about that guy or girl you keep saying is just a friend. Not every relationship has a happy ending. And the ones that do work require a hell of a lot of grit and determination. Dreams can come true but they are far from the idealistically applied views we are conditioned to believe. The desire to be loved is universal. However, there is no formula, love serum or game play that can lead to the perfect relationship.

Love never has and never will come easy.

10219727R00066

Printed in Germany
by Amazon Distribution
GmbH, Leipzig